Tax Strategies

*How to Outsmart the System and the IRS
as a Real Estate Investor by Increasing
Your Income and Lowering Your Taxes by
Investing Smarter*

Volume 1

By

Income Mastery

her competence. There are no scenarios in which the publisher or author of this book can be held responsible for any difficulties or damages that may occur to them after using the information presented here.

In addition, the information on the following pages is intended for informational purposes only and should therefore be regarded as universal. As befits its nature, it is presented without warranty with respect to its prolonged validity or provisional quality. The trademarks mentioned are made without written consent and can in no way be considered as sponsorship of the same.

TABLE OF CONTENTS

Chapter 1: The Origin of Taxes

Brief History on Taxes

Throughout history and the passing of time of what we call civilization we find that since the first forms of social organization that were established, the figure of taxes has existed, and they were set according to their type and forms. This was at the discretion of the sovereigns or regents who were mostly part of their tributes, many of which were intended for ceremonial matters and directed to the expenses of the most dominant classes in their time.

"Cheating" on taxes was really difficult and uncommon at those times, due to the direct control made by priests and sovereigns over collection of taxes. It is interesting to note that among some very old texts in cuneiform writing, known as the ancient writing cast on clay tablets of about five thousand years ago, it was written that "you can love a prince, you can love a king, but before a tax at the front of a tax collector, you should tremble," always making a direct reference to the collection of taxes.

Similarly, we can find in the history of ancient civilizations such as Egypt, China and Mesopotamia that in these places appeared the first rules of taxation with the appearance of the first tax laws and were characterized by being very old texts.

A common way to comply with the tribute in Egypt was through physical work, in this way different pyramids were built as that of King Cheops in the year 2,500 B.C. the same one that lasted twenty years more, participating approximately 100,000 people who moved materials from Ethiopia to the place where the construction would be done. It is also found in an inscription of a tomb of Sakkara with an antiquity of approximately 2,300 years B.C. the one dealing with a tax return on animals, fruits and others alike.

On the other hand, in this same kingdom the people had to kneel before Pharaoh's tax collectors, who besides presenting their declaration, had to ask for graces for all the services they rendered. Ceramic pieces at the time were used as tax receipts. On the Mediterranean island of Crete, in the second millennium BC, King Minos received even human beings as a tribute. In China, Confucius was Prince Dschau's tax inspector in Lu state in 532 B.C. Lao Tse said that the people could not be well directed because of excessive tax burdens.

In the particular case of Latin America, one can prove the payment of tax through the shipments that Spanish settlers made in gold, precious stones and food to the monarchs who were in Europe as a form of royalties during the time of colonization of the Spanish conquistadors in the new continent.

In pre-Columbian Mexico, it was customary to give the Aztecs rubber balls, eagles, snakes, and annually young men whose hearts were torn out as part of their religious ceremonies. The collection of taxes and tributes, also had its eccentric things and in some dark cases, it is known that the king Azcapotzalco in one occasion, asked the Aztecs that separately from the raft sowed with flowers and fruits that they gave him as tribute, they also should take him a heron and a duck laying on their eggs, in such a way that when they received them they were stinging the shell.

The Aztecs improved their technique of taxation, they used the calpixquis, called like this representing the figures in charge of collecting taxes, which carried as a distinctive sign or credential a rod in one hand and a spectrum in the other and were dedicated to collecting taxes. They imposed heavy burdens on the defeated peoples, a situation that was established in the pre and post court codices, which show the infinity of objects, natural products such as cotton and precious metals that were used as tributes. The Mendocino Code tells us that taxes were also paid with processed articles such as fabrics, in addition to the existence of a register (registration of taxes). Later, the tribute in kind of the Aztecs was replaced by the collection of taxes in coins by the Spanish government.

In Peru, the collection of taxes for the Incas consisted on people offering what they produced with their own hands to the king god, who in exchange gave them what they needed for their subsistence, supported, of course, by an army of officials. The Incas used color-knotted ropes (depending on the tax) called "quipos", which were knotted according to their amount. The processes were so complicated that the assistance of tax advisors called "quipos-camayos" had to be requested for all their preparation and collection.

As can be seen, in ancient times, the way to pay and collect taxes was not entirely equitable and was rather due to situations of whim, divine mandate or subjugation of one people by another with the sole purpose of satisfying themselves. We can also see that the same human beings were part of the tributes and were destined for ceremonial sacrifices or forced to perform physical labor. Some tax returns were humiliating, because when they were filed, the taxpayer had to kneel down and ask for thanks.

Now, as you can compare, taxes are handled very differently, mainly because taxes are a form of compulsory contribution made by citizens of a country to its government. This is in order for the State to obtain the income that is necessary to fully develop its functions in terms of issues such as education, health, food, state security, among many other projects aimed at benefiting its population of interest.

Chapter 2: Taxes and Its Types

To be able to define what taxes are, it is necessary and important to know and understand that not all taxes are the same for everyone, since the amount that must be paid in taxes varies depending on some characteristics such as how much income and assets the people or companies that must pay these taxes have. Taxes are also known as benefits or taxes, it is understood as mandatory contributions that generally must be made through payments in cash or through your debit or credit cards depending on the type of payment they accept, such payments are sent to the State as a government entity that regulates such contributions to be administered by national public law entities created for this purpose, which are responsible for claiming such contributions from each of us.

In this sense the taxes are mandatory, that is to say that its fulfillment in a forced form and it is not going to depend on your discretion or decision, in definitive it is a duty that you must fulfill and its form and amount are determined unilaterally by the State and without special consideration with the purpose of satisfying the collective needs.

In fact, the tax is a compulsory tax benefit, the budget of which is not an activity of the State referring to the obligor and intended to cover public expenses, but the tax itself is the representation of the benefit of money or similar established by the State in accordance with the law, with obligatory character, at the expense of physical and moral persons to cover the public expense and without there being for them any special, direct and immediate consideration or benefit. That is to say that you will not be able to decide the immediate and specific destination for which your tax is going to be used, this is a privileged and exclusive decision of the national State of your country.

In the economic sphere, tribute is understood as a type of contribution that all citizens must pay to the State in order to redistribute them equitably or according to the needs of the moment. Except in some cases, taxes are paid through cash benefits and can be grouped into three categories: taxes, contributions and fees.

Types of taxes

There are two main types of taxes at the time of classifying them: direct taxes and indirect taxes, without forgetting that there are other types of taxes which we will mention later.

- Direct taxes: we are going to understand that they are all those taxes that fall, in a direct way, on the person, company or society, among others; these are based on the economic capacity of the same ones, the obtaining of rents and the patrimonies that possess. Among the most common direct taxes are personal income tax and corporate income tax.

- Indirect taxes: Unlike direct taxes, indirect taxes are those that are imposed on goods and services, as well as on the transactions that are made with them, in other words, each time a person makes the purchase of a good or service, he or she is paying a tax indirectly. This type of tax is not paid directly by the specific person but falls on that good or service that is acquired. Among the most common indirect taxes are the Value Added Tax (VAT), the special tax on alcoholic beverages and the tax on capital transfers.

Other taxes: When we refer to other types of taxes, we refer to progressive taxes, regressive taxes and proportional taxes, these have their own protocol of application and will have a different incidence following the tax patterns and models of each country, but in general terms within this classification can be explained in the following way:

- Proportional Taxes: Taxes whose assessment is calculated as a fixed percentage, such as VAT, regardless of the income of the individual who must pay the tax.

- Regressive taxes: Taxes where the higher the income the lower the percentage of tax, such as VAT on basic goods.

- Progressive taxes: These are those taxes in which the greater the income or gain that is received, the greater the percentage of taxes that must be paid, such as that applied to the income of natural or juridical persons.

What are the kinds of tributes?

According to tax laws in general, taxes are tolls levied without consideration, whose taxable event is constituted by businesses, acts or facts of a legal or economic nature that show the taxpayer's contributive capacity as a consequence of the possession of a patrimony, the circulation of goods or the acquisition or expense of income. In other words, taxes are payments that are made because they show the capacity to face public administration expenses.

Taxes can be classified under:

- Direct Taxes (such as Income Tax or ISR) and Indirect Taxes (such as Value Added Tax or VAT).

- Personal Taxes (because the taxpayer pays for his global capacity) and Real Taxes (the taxpayer pays for a fact that demonstrates his capacity).

- Taxes Objectives (do not consider the taxpayer's capacity) and Subjective (do consider the taxpayer's capacity).

Periodic Taxes (paid more than once in time) and Instantaneous Taxes (paid once for some facts).

A key figure in understanding the concept of tax is the taxable event, in this context, it is the circumstance or the de facto budget (of a legal or economic nature), established by law to configure each tax, the performance of which gives rise to the birth of the main tax obligation, i.e. the payment of the tax. For example, obtaining income is the taxable event in the Personal Income Tax or the possession of a real estate, the Real Estate Tax.

It is important to consider that there are some taxes that must be paid at the national or federal level, while others are the responsibility of the Local Treasuries, so it is important to be well informed about these details when paying the corresponding taxes, in order to avoid unnecessary problems and complications in any case.

Chapter 3: General Concepts to Know

Who are the taxpayers and what are their obligations?

Now, in this intricate world of taxes, tributes or in its diversity of expression we find the figure of the taxpayer. Taxpayers are no more than citizens, in short, people who, in their capacity as natural or legal persons, must pay the respective taxes that they have to face according to their required condition or circumstance; in short, the taxpayer is the one who pays taxes to the State.

In this way, it is important that taxpayers observe and take consider some aspects to comply with the obligations that they have to comply with, therefore, keeping the accounting of their operations, separating those taxed and exempt and those that do not give rise to accreditation is of great benefit and often even a tax requirement.

For the above described we will point out some of the aspects that should be considered by the taxpayer for the organized planning of the payment of their taxes:

- The taxpayer must always issue documents that prove the value of the agreed contract, indicating expressly and separately the value added tax that is transferred. These documents must be delivered to the acquirer within fifteen calendar days of the transaction.

- When filing returns, taxpayers with multiple establishments must file a single return.

- Taxpayers must obtain and safeguard for future use the vouchers where the VAT is transferred separately.

- Tax brokers will separate their accounts from those of other registries. Therefore, taxpayers must deliver the documentation in the order and manner intended by the collecting and taxing institutions.

- The taxpayer must have the VAT included in the price when dealing with the general public.

- Taxpayers must keep in each establishment a copy of all payment statements made.

- All taxpayers who at any time enjoy the benefit of withholdings must issue evidence by effect of the withholdings obtained.

Active Subject vs Passive Subject

After knowing what taxes are about and understanding the figure of the taxpayer, we must also know what is known as subjects of the tax, in the understanding that the first element that intervenes in a tax relationship is the subject. The subject is of two classes, an active subject and a passive subject.

Within the organization of the States, the active subjects are the Governorates or Federal States, the Local Entities as mayors or city councils and the Municipalities with their councilors.

That is to say, all those representatives of the government are active subjects before the right that their investiture gives them to demand the payment of taxes; but not all taxes are going to have the same amplitude and extension. All the national or national institutions will have those constitutional limitations that are so defined and specifically contained in each magna charter of a country, therefore, such institutions after taking care of such precepts may establish the taxes, they deem necessary to cover their budgets. On the other hand, the Municipality only has the faculty to collect them except in those cases where the constitution admits it.

Bearing in mind the difference explained, we can say that national governments as well as federal and local entities have full tax sovereignty. Municipalities have subordinate tax sovereignty.

Now, when we speak of a taxpayer, this is the person who legally has the obligation to pay the tax, that is, we as taxpayers who, as citizens who live a social and common life, have the obligation to contribute to the plenipotentiary development of our country and to the improvement of public services, duly paying our income tax ISR or value-added tax IVA and any other tax determined by law according to the work we are doing (such as selling a property, renting or leasing a property).

Chapter 4: Value Added Tax or VAT?

Now when we enter into the subject of VAT, we already know that there is a very diverse variety of tax types but if one of them stands out for its wide use and direct effect on the common of citizens is the so-called value added tax commonly known by the acronym VAT. This tax is part of the group of sales taxes, directly affects the consumer through industrialists and traders, everything we acquire through the purchase of an object presents this type of tax as a value added to the price. Because the value-added tax apparently taxes the industrial and trader's income, when in reality what it reflects is the consumer's expenditure and directly the real price and the price paid for the purposes of the tax paid.

The State considers that regardless of the profits that the individual may obtain from his activity, there is the benefit that the individual derives from the action of the State, aimed at the provision of public services and for which he must pay in order to support the expenses that those public services demand.

This means that by the action of the State, the individual derives two kinds of benefits: one that is represented by the use that he can make of the services that the State provides and the other by the profit that can derive from the activity that he carries out within the legal world in which he moves, within the limits and under the protection of the State.

The Value Added Tax known universally by its initials IVA abrogates or substitutes, among others, the federal tax on mercantile income, whose main deficiency was that it was caused in a "cascade", that is to say, that it had to be paid in each one of the stages of production and commercialization, which determined in all of them an increase in costs and prices, an increase whose cumulative effects, in short, affected the final consumers.

However, the purpose for which VAT was implemented has been to eliminate the harmful results of the federal or government tax on mercantile income, since it destroys the cumulative cascade effect and the influence it exerts on general price levels. That is, if this tax goes directly to the taxpayer, that is to say, it is a direct tax that we, as citizens have to pay for purchasing a product.

This is how the intention of the VAT is not to harm nor does it intend to tax the utility of the companies, what affects is the global, real and definitive value of each product through the imposition on the different partial values of each producer, manufacturer, wholesaler, retailer is incorporating the article in each stage of the negotiation of the goods, both in the industrial cycle and in the commercial cycle, they are producers of wealth and must be consequently, taxed with this type of tax.

Without overlooking the fact that value-added tax or VAT is also paid at each stage of production, it does not produce cumulative effects, since each industry or trader, upon receiving payment of the tax it transfers to its clients, recovers the tax its suppliers would have passed on to it, and only delivers the difference to the State; in this way, the system does not allow the tax paid at each stage to influence the cost of goods and services, and when these reach the final consumer they do not hide any tax burden in the price.

In the same way, the value added tax or VAT that is paid in some countries is an indirect tax, that is to say, it is paid by a person who has not only the right but also the obligation to transfer it, so that in the end it is paid by the consumer. It is real because the taxable event does not consider the personal conditions of the taxpayers, but only the nature of the economic operations.

Who are the Subjects of the Value Added Tax or VAT?

We understand those individuals and companies legally obliged to pay this tax. In most countries, the payment of value added tax or VAT is mandatory for natural and legal persons who, in their national territory, perform acts or activities related to the performance of the following activities:

1. Disposal of assets.

2. Provision of independent services.

3. To grant the temporary use or enjoyment of goods.

4. Import goods or services.

5. Export of goods or services.

In this sense it is pertinent that we know what it means or how each one of the actions or acts that were previously indicated are interpreted:

1. What do we mean by alienation?

Disposal is understood to be any transfer of ownership of property, with the exception of that carried out by cause of death or by merger of companies. For example, the donation is considered a taxable disposition when it is made by companies for which the donation is not deductible for income tax purposes.

We must also understand it as an activity of alienation:

- The sale in which the seller reserves ownership of the property sold since the conclusion of the contract, even if the transfer operates later, or fails to take place.

- Awards, even if they are made in favor of the creditor.

- The contribution to a society, foundation or association.

- That which is carried out through financial leasing.

Exemptions or privileges for payments of value added tax or VAT.

No tax is paid on the disposal of the following assets:

- The floor

- Constructions attached to the ground, intended or used for habitation. When only part of the property is used for housing, no tax is payable on that part. Hotels are not included in this fraction due to their nature as a for-profit company.

- Books, newspapers and magazines, as well as the right to exploit a work by its author.

- Used movable property, with the exception of property disposed of by companies.

- Tickets and other vouchers that allow participation in lotteries, raffles, sweepstakes or games with bets and contests, as well as the respective prizes referred to in the Income Tax Law or ISR.

- National and foreign currency, as well as gold or silver pieces that had such a character and the pieces called "troy ounce".

- Gold bullion with a minimum content of 99% of such material, provided that it is sold in retail sales to the general public.

Disposal is deemed to have taken place in any of the following cases:

- From the moment the good is sent or delivered to the buyer.

- As long as the price of the good is paid in full or in part.

- From the moment the document protecting the alienation is issued.

2. What is independent service provision?

They are considered independent services:

- The provision of obligations to make one person perform in favor of another, whatever the act that gives rise to it and the name or classification given to such act by other laws.

- The transport of goods or people.

- Insurance, bonding and refinancing.

- The mandate, commission, mediation, agency, representation, brokerage, consignment and distribution.

- Technical assistance and technology transfer.

- Any other obligation to give, not to do or to permit, assumed by one person for the benefit of another, provided that it is not considered by this law as a temporary alienation or use or enjoyment of property.

The tax is not paid for the provision of the following services:

- Those provided directly by the Federation, DF, States and Municipalities that do not correspond to their functions of public law.

- Those provided by public social security institutions.

- Fees and considerations covered by the borrower to his creditor for the granting of mortgage loans.

- The commissions charged for the administration of their resources.

- Free services.

- Educational services.

- Public land transport of persons, except railways.

- The international maritime transport of goods provided by residents abroad without permanent establishment in the country.

- Those of maquila of flour or dough, of corn or wheat.

- People in charge of milk pasteurization.

- Insurance against agricultural risks and life insurance, whether they cover the risk of death or grant annuities or pensions, as well as agent commissions corresponding to the aforementioned insurance.

- Derivative financial transactions.

- Services provided to its members, political parties, associations, coalitions, trade unions, chambers of commerce, employers' associations and professional associations.

- Those of public spectacles for the entrance ticket. A public spectacle is not considered to be a spectacle borrowed in restaurants, bars, cabarets, ballrooms and nightclubs.

3. What is called temporary use or enjoyment of property?

The temporary use or enjoyment of goods is understood to be the lease, usufruct and any other act, regardless of the legal form used for this purpose, whereby one person allows another to use or temporarily enjoy tangible goods in exchange for a consideration.

Exemptions:

The tax will not be paid in the following cases:

- Buildings intended or used exclusively for habitation. If a property has several uses, the part proportional to the house will be taxed.

- Farms for agricultural or livestock purposes.

- Tangible goods whose enjoyment is granted by residents abroad without permanent establishment in national territory.

- Books, newspapers and magazines.

4. What are imported goods?

The importation of goods is considered to be any product of any characteristic that is introduced in the territory of a nation, that is, that its origin is external to the national production, in such sense the tax rates that will be applied concern:

- The introduction of foreign goods into the country.

- The acquisition by persons residing in the country of tangible goods disposed of by persons not residing in the country.

- The temporary use or enjoyment, in the national territory, of intangible goods provided by persons not residing therein.

- The temporary use or enjoyment, in the national territory, of the services referred to in the previous topic, when they are provided by non-residents in the country. This part does not apply to international transport.

Exemptions.

- Those that are not consummated, are temporary, have the character of return of goods temporarily exported or are the object of transit or transshipment.

- The luggage and household materials referred to in the customs code.

- Goods donated by residents abroad to the Federation, States, Municipalities according to the general rules established for this purpose by the Secretariat of Finance and Public Credit.

5. *What do we call export of goods or services?*

This defines the economic activity that people, or companies carry out outside their country even if they have tax residence in their country of origin. The company's resident in the country will pay the tax on the sale of goods or services when one or the other exports the products or services that they have to develop. In such a way that the taxpayers will be obliged to pay taxes in the following cases:

- The transaction of intangible assets by persons residing in the country to those residing abroad.

- The temporary use or enjoyment, abroad, of intangible property provided by persons residing in the country.

- The use abroad of services rendered by residents of the country for: a) technical assistance, b) export measurement operations, c) advertising, d) commissions and mediation, e) insurance and reinsurance, f) financing operations.

- The international transportation of goods provided by residents in the country.

- The air transport of persons, provided by the resident in the country, by that part of the service which is not considered to be provided in the national territory.

The exporter may choose between crediting or refunding the amounts paid on the goods or services exported, even when they are exempt items, or when company's resident in the country export tangible goods in order to transfer them or to grant their use or enjoyment abroad.

Chapter 5: Income Tax or ISR

What is Income Tax (ISR)? a question that many people ask themselves, but everyone has to pay.

To understand this type of direct tax that most taxpayers pay, we must know:

What is known as Income Tax?

Income is the product of capital, labor or the combination of capital and labor. For tax purposes, a distinction can be made between gross income, which is the total income received without any deduction, such as when a tax is levied on income from work or derived from capital in the form of interest. Other times the free income is taxed when, after deducting from the income the expenses necessary to obtain the income, the deduction of certain particular expenses of the taxable person is also allowed.

Who is called a Subject?

It is called subject to all individuals and companies that must pay ISR for:

- National residents according to their annual income.

- Residents abroad who have a permanent establishment or a fixed base in the country, in respect of the income attributable to that establishment or base. Likewise, those whose income comes from sources within the national territory and who do not have a permanent establishment and, where one exists, that the income is not attributable to them.

What is a Permanent Establishment?

Any place of business in which business activities are carried out (branches, agencies, offices, workshops, facilities, mines, place of exploration, exploitation or extraction of natural resources).

What is the Income of a business establishment?

They are those coming from the developed business activity, those coming from fees and those that derive from the rendering of an independent personal service. Also, for the transaction of goods or real estate on national territory.

Who is a Moral Person according to the different legislations on the income tax or ISR?

Companies, decentralized bodies with business activity, credit institutions, societies and civil associations are considered legal persons. Corporate entities will pay income tax on the result of applying 35% to the taxable income obtained in the year.

What is the Tax Result about?

- Tax profit is obtained by reducing the total accumulated income obtained in the year by the deductions authorized by law.

- Tax loss carryforwards from other years will be deducted from taxable income for the year.

What is known as a Partial Exemption?

Partial exemption shall be granted to legal persons engaged exclusively in agricultural, livestock, forestry or fishing activities, provided that their income in the financial year does not exceed the amount of high general minimum wages per year established by the tax legislation of each country.

This exemption will have a maximum that can exceed and in the total number of times also designated by the tax authorities of each country.

In addition, they will not pay ISR for their products:

- Ejidos.

- Unions of ejidos.

- Social enterprises.

- Rural associations of collective interest.

- Industrial agricultural unit for peasant women.

- Agricultural and cattle colonies.

What is the tax-reducing activities?

Reduction of the tax will be granted in the following cases and with average percentages in different countries:

- The activities dedicated to agriculture, livestock, fishing or forestry, can obtain from 50 to 75% in tax reduction depending on the economic policy of the country.

- If these taxpayers industrialize their products, they can obtain a 50 to 25% reduction in their taxes depending on the production and development plans of each country.

- If they carry out commercial or industrial activities in which they have a maximum of 30% of their income, they can obtain a 15 to 25% reduction in their tax as determined by the tax law of the nation.

- In the case of the edition of books, magazines and any other editorial product can be obtained from 25% to 75% depending on the purpose of publication. Obtaining, of course, the greatest tax reductions of an educational nature.

Taxpayers of this type are those whose income from their activities represents at least 90% of their total income.

What do we know by Income?

Moral persons shall accumulate all the income in cash, goods, service, credit or any other type that they obtain in the fiscal year, including those coming from their establishments abroad. In short, it is any collection obtained from the loan of a service or transaction of a commercial or mercantile nature.

The inflationary gain is the income that taxpayers obtain from the real reduction of their debts.

The following are considered cumulative income:

- Certain income determined by entities issuing income tax.

- The difference between the part of the investment not yet deducted, updated according to the law and the value that according to the appraisal made by a person authorized by the entity issuing the tax has on the date on which your property is transferred for payment in kind.

- Difference between inventories in the case of stockbreeders. The difference between the final and initial inventories of a fiscal year, when the final inventory is the largest in the case of taxpayers dedicated to livestock.

- Benefit for improvements that pass to the landlord. Those that come from constructions, installations or permanent improvements in real estate, that in accordance with the contracts for which their use or enjoyment was granted are for the benefit of the owner.

- Gain on disposal of assets, securities, merger, spin-off, etc.

- Payments for recovery of a credit deducted for uncollectible.

- Recovery for insurance, bonds. Et cetera.

- Insurance indemnity income from the key man. The amounts that the taxpayer obtains as compensation to compensate for the decrease in productivity caused by the death, accident or illness of technicians or managers.

- Interest and inflationary gain.

Regarding deductions, taxpayers may make the following deductions:

- Returns, discounts or bonuses. Even if they are carried out in subsequent years.

- Acquisition of goods, as well as raw materials, semi-finished or finished products used to provide services, to manufacture goods, to dispose of them, reduced by returns, discounts and rebates on the same carried out even in subsequent years.

- Expenses.

- Investments.

- Difference in inventories in the case of cattle breeders.

- Bad debts and fortuitous losses.

- Contributions to funds for technology and training (Art. 27).

- Creation of reserves for pension funds, retirements, etc.

- Interest and inflationary loss.

- Advances and yields paid by cooperative production societies, as well as advances given by societies and civil associations to their members.

What is meant by Fixed Assets, Expenses and Deferred Charges?

Investments are considered fixed assets, expenses and deferred charges, to better understand them we will say that:

FIXED ASSETS:

They are a set of tangible goods that taxpayers use to carry out their activities and that are demerited by the use in the taxpayer's service and by the passage of time. The acquisition or manufacture of these goods shall always have the purpose of using them for the development of the taxpayer's activities, and not of being disposed of within the normal course of their operations.

DEFERRED EXPENDITURE:

These are intangible assets represented by goods or rights that make it possible to reduce operating costs, or improve the quality or acceptance of a product, for a limited period, less than the duration of the activity of the legal entity. Deferred expenses also include intangible assets that permit the exploitation of public property or the provision of a public service concession.

THE DEFERRED CHARGES:

They are those that meet the requirements indicated in the previous paragraph. Except those relating to the exploitation of goods in the public domain or the provision of a public service concession, but whose benefit is for an unlimited period depending on the duration of the activity of the legal person.

Some of the obligations that Moral Persons have are the following:

- Keeping records.

- Issue receipts for the operations carried out.

- Formulate financial statements and make inventories.

- File an annual return.

- Keep track of transactions with securities issued in series.

- Keep supporting documentation.

On the other hand, these are the obligations of Physical Persons:

- Income tax or ISR is paid by all persons residing in the nation.

- Foreign residents with business activities or who provide independent personal services in the country.

The exemptions in the payment of the income tax or ISR, can be in the cases of:

- Non-wage and overtime benefits.

- Compensation for risks or illnesses.

- Retirements, pensions and retirement assets.

- Reimbursement of medical, dental, hospital and funeral expenses.

- Social security benefit and social security.

- Delivery of a deposit to the institute responsible for social security or any other denomination given to it in each country.

39

- Workers' savings banks and funds.

- IMSS fee.

- Seniority, retirement and severance bonuses (90 times SMG x each year of service).

- Bonuses, holiday bonuses and OCTs (15 times SMG).

- Remunerations received by foreigners.

- Representation expenses and per diem.

- Frozen rents.

- Disposal of the house provided that it is proven that the house was occupied in the last two years prior to the disposal.

- Agricultural, livestock, forestry or fishing activities (20 times MGA per year).

- Interest paid by credit institutions provided they are savings deposits made in an amount not exceeding the equivalent of twice the annual MGA.

- Interest received by international credit institutions.

- Interest on bonds issued by the Federal Government.

- Interest derived from insurance institutions.

- Inheritance or legacy.

- Donations (Sponsorship service, maximum 3 to 4 times a year according to state legislation).

- Compensation for damages.

- Food.

- Copyrights.

- Wage Income (Subordinate Person Service).

They are the duty of the Subjects:

- To provide data for the inscription in the register of treasury or fiscal collection of goods destined each country for such purpose.

- Request withholding tax records.

- File an annual return.

- Communicate in writing when working for two or more patterns.

They are the obligation of the Patrons:

- Withhold ISR.

- Calculate the annual tax.

- Provide records to workers no later than 31 January.

- Ask for records when the worker worked for other employers.

- Ask the worker to tell you if he or she has worked for another employer.

- Submit annual return for wages paid.

- Request data from workers in order to register them in the national tax registration system.

Chapter 6: What Are Tax Reductions?

On one hand, tax reductions are changes in tax legislation that effectively reduce the amount of taxes you have to pay, these kinds of established changes have a negative effect on taxes, but positive in terms of the money we have to invest in it.

The term "tax reduction" may seem a little difficult to understand and often confusing, because it is a broad term covering a diverse range of situations that result in a lower amount of tax collected by the government. The only thing all tax cuts have in common is that they modify a pre-existing tax law or implement a new one that effectively reduces the amount of taxes you have to pay.

On the other hand, we must bear in mind that taxpayers can reduce their taxes to the extent that we take precautions and organize ourselves in such a way that our income is not affected by the payment of too many taxes. That is why we have prepared a complete chapter for this purpose.

What are Income Tax Rate Reductions?

In some countries, cuts or reductions in the payment of income tax have been decreed as transitional measures in the form of presidential decrees or resolutions issued by congresses or tax entities in their power for such purposes. In these cases, the effect is very wide of the income tax reduction, as all taxpayers will benefit automatically.

In this sense we can give as an example the American case of 2017, where the lowest tax rate charged by the U.S. government was 10 percent. If this changed the following year to reach 8 percent, then Congress would have issued a tax cut. To illustrate it better, suppose you declare taxes as a single taxpayer and have $8,000 of taxable income. Using the 10 percent rate, you'll have to pay $800 in income tax. However, after a tax reduction, you will only have pay US$640.

What are Temporary Tax Cuts?

In some cases, governments reduce taxes for a specific period of time to stimulate the economy with a tax cut that disappears in the next fiscal year.

A perfect example is the temporary reduction of the Social Security tax rate issued by the State of Mexico from 6.2 percent to 4.2 percent during fiscal year 2012.

However, in 2013 and beyond, the rate returned to 6.2 percent. Similarly, in 2009 Congress allowed those receiving unemployment compensation to exclude the first $2,400 from taxable income. Beginning in 2011, this $2,400 exclusion is no longer available, and you must report 100 percent of your unemployment compensation on your tax return.

What is the expansion of tax rate ranges about?

Most governments that charge an income tax use a progressive tax system. That is, they use different tax rates depending on the specific range of income. Instead of making a tax reduction with a reduction in tax rates, a similar result can be obtained if the range of income subject to the lowest tax rates increases.

For example, if ISR imposes taxes at a rate of 10 percent on the first US$9,325 of profits. If the 10 percent collection range increases to $12,000 of initial income, this tax cut can save you a significant amount of money, since a smaller proportion of your income will be subject to tax in the higher ranges.

What is known as increased limits on deductions?

Most of the deductions you can claim have limitations on the amount you can deduct or the maximum income you can earn to be eligible to claim it.

For example, when you detail your deductions, you can include the portion of medical expenses that exceeds a total of 7.5 percent of your adjusted gross income (AGI) for 2017 and 2018. However, if Congress ever decides to reduce this limitation to GAI or eliminate it altogether, this will effectively be a tax reduction because the end result is that you will pay less taxes by being able to claim a larger deduction.

In preparing to modify the nation's fiscal code, government or federal legislators must consider a fundamental question: What are the priorities for tax reform? Is faster growth sought? Less income inequality? A tax cut that does not raise the budget deficit. Depending on how this tax cut is targeted, some progress can be made towards the first two objectives. Reducing personal income tax can help support growth and, if it is well-targeted, it can also help to improve income distribution. However, we observe that lowering tax rates does not enhance growth sufficiently to compensate for the loss of tax revenue caused precisely by the tax reduction itself.

The tax reform debate is ongoing as the U.S. economy experiences one of the longest periods of expansion in its history. In the medium term, however, growth prospects are constrained by weak productivity growth, declining labor force participation, and an increasingly polarized income distribution.

Finding solutions to these problems requires action in many areas, such as trade, education and health. In the last assessment of the US economy, the IMF and the US authorities also mentioned tax policy as an important instrument. Our paper looks more closely at the notion that tax reforms, and personal income tax cuts in particular, can go a long way towards meeting these challenges. But how much can a tax reduction really help? Can a reduction in personal income tax boost growth? And if so, can you raise it enough not to generate a burden on the budget? More importantly, will the benefits of reform reach low- and middle-income households?

Evaluating the dynamic effects of a reduction in the effective rate of income tax or income tax of individuals on the distribution of income and the economy in any country is of real importance given the direct impact it will have both on our income and on the annual collection made by the treasury of our nation for the benefit of all citizens.

For this evaluation of the reduction of the effective rate of income tax or SRI, modern tools of quantitative macroeconomic analysis are used, based on a model that gathers the most outstanding characteristics of each nation that are essential for the issue of tax reduction, that is, indicators are used such as different types of households (differentiated by educational level), different productive sectors (manufacturing and services) interrelated through a realistic structure of input-output, and international trade.

Moreover, unlike conventional incidence analyses, this approach incorporates prospective dynamics and behaviors, allowing us to consider the medium-term effects of policy changes.

Chapter 7: Income Tax /ISR – Reduction vs Deduction

I suppose we all know the importance of taxes for the operative of a nation, understanding that this contribution allows the improvement of services and projects of common interest, but it is also important that the payment of tax is not unfavorable to our own interests and cover our needs so we must be aware of the process involved in paying our ISR without this resulting in an unfavorable way and not paying more.

For when we are in the process of preparing our income tax return, we have considered it appropriate to clarify two terms that are often confused when it comes to conceptualizing the idea of paying less taxes for certain tax benefits: deductions and reductions.

As a common feature, both reductions and tax deductions have the final result of either increasing the amount of ISR returned to us or reducing the amount to be paid, depending on whether the result is to be paid or to be returned. That is to say, in both cases we will be benefiting economically from its application in our income tax return.

TAX REDUCTIONS:

They have a direct impact on the tax base on which the resulting income tax liability is calculated. As a general rule, the reductions relate to expenses associated with obtaining income: fees to professional associations, contributions to social welfare, etc.

A clear example of how reductions work when calculating the ISR is the concept known as "personal and family minimum", which subtracts from the taxable base an amount considered the minimum necessary to cover basic needs according to the circumstances of each taxpayer. The application of this concept implies that, for example, a minimum amount is always deducted from the total value (in your local currency) before the application of the tax rate that will give the contribution to be paid.

TAX DEDUCTIONS:

Once we have applied the percentages corresponding to the taxable base (subtracting all the reductions), we will know the figure known as the integral quota, which is the one we would have to pay (or receive) if it were not for the existence of another type of tax benefits, known as tax deductions.

Unlike reductions, tax deductions often respond to a political will to promote certain aspects, such as maternity, the rehabilitation of habitual housing, patronage or any other form of social protection.

The amounts of the tax deductions are directly subtracted from the total amount of tax to be paid, having a direct effect on the amount that we will receive or finally pay. For example, if our quota without deductions is raised to a payment of US$1500 , and we apply a tax deduction of US$2000 for rehabilitation of the habitual residence, at the end our income tax return will result in a refund in our favor of US$500.

There are deductions at state and regional level, and it is important to know which ones we can opt for their particular conditions (limits, requirements or conditions that are foreseen). If you make an erroneous deduction, you will be forced to repay the amount with interests.

On the other hand, it is not too much to know the arguments presented by the International Monetary Fund (IMF) according to the reduction of taxes in a governmental way as mechanisms for the increase of citizen participation, with this purpose and for these effects the IMF presents in its blog the following three general arguments that according to them have to be considered by the nations that require their economic aid or financing which are presented from three points of analysis, which refer to:

- As for the reduction of taxes to give impulse to the increase of Gross Domestic Product (GDP), the following stands out: although we were able

51

to determine that the reduction of taxes generates for once an impulse to GDP, consumption and investment, these effects are never powerful enough to prevent a loss of fiscal income. Therefore, tax cuts would have to be financed either by increasing public debt, lowering expenditure or by raising revenue through other taxes. Since our objective is to achieve better distributional outcomes while preserving the possibility of achieving some moderate increase in growth, we focus on the shift from personal income taxes to consumption taxes as a means of financing the cut, combined with an expansion of the earned income tax credit to protect the poor.

- The tax cuts are equivalent to the substantial benefit to the people: we note that the reduction in personal income tax can benefit lower income groups, even if those at the bottom of the income scale do not directly receive such a cut. Our economic model predicts that when tax cuts are targeted at middle (or upper) income groups, these groups will spend part of their tax savings on (non-tradable) services, which are commonly provided by lower income people. Richer groups, on average, devote a larger proportion of their consumption expenditure to services. Consequently, when wealthier people pay less tax, their spending on services increases, thus raising demand and wages for low-skilled labor.

- Reducing taxes reduces income inequality: IMF analysis reveals a fundamental trade-off between growth and income inequality, depending on who receives the tax cut. In our simulations, while tax reductions in favor of higher income groups may be more beneficial to GDP by increasing investment and labor supply, they also exacerbate polarization and income inequality, variables that are already at historical highs. Even considering that the rich could consume more goods and services produced by people at the bottom of the income distribution, and even if an increase in the labor income tax credit is envisaged to protect the poor, the income gap would still widen substantially if taxes were reduced for higher income groups. On the other hand, a tax cut aimed at middle-income groups would reduce income disparity and polarization, but its contribution to growth could be less.

Chapter 8: Planning Your Income Tax Return for Possible Tax Reductions

We all know what happens once a year when the majority of the population in all parts of the world prepares to make their balance sheets to be prepared at the time of making the payment of their taxes, uncertainty and running looking for the last statement gives us an endless unnecessary anxiety but if we planned ahead we could save that discomfort.

Therefore, it is best to start planning your taxes with the following suggestions, which will benefit substantially in reducing the payment of your income tax or ISR:

- Let's start with one of the possible tax breaks; do you work from home? Even if you don't do it all the time, it's possible to deduct part of your household expenses, i.e. alleviating the costs of paying for a lease or extra property to do your work also reduces service taxes or some other tax required for commercial or mercantile use.

- Another reduction that we sometimes forget is the cost of transportation and travel. If you are going to deduct entertainment expenses, remember to save the receipt and write down the exact names and reason.

- We continue with credits, if you used credit to finance something in your business, the interest you paid is completely deductible. If you replaced a computer or equipment you no longer use, remember to donate it to a charity and get a deduction.

- And if you are lucky enough to have an entrepreneur child, hire them and you will be able to pay them a considerable amount that can range from 5% to 10% tax free. Take advantage and convince them to invest their earnings in a Roth IRA, where they will grow tax-free and will be able to settle at 59 1/12 without any penalty or tax. Remember that if you have a corporation, you can only partially save taxes.

- Would you rather give your money to the government or your retirement? Invest in yours and your employees retirement. Most retirement plans allow your money to grow tax-free and you'll also have the ability to deduct the amount from your business profits. You can contribute to this, for example, if you are over 50, or if you employ people with a functional disability. There are other types of retirement plans to which you can contribute. Also, consider plans where you can contribute tax-free to your health.

If you are thinking of changing your entity, consider a corporation as a nongovernmental organization or foundation and you can save on payroll taxes. In some countries amounts like these will have a tax of up to 2.9%. With a nongovernmental organization or foundation, the increments can be saved.

- If you can't do your annual income tax or ISR planning on your own, get help. Whether it's buying an advanced tax program, hiring an accountant or using a college intern, whatever your strategy is, it's better that you have someone to organize your expenses and your accounting. You must guarantee the reliability of the medium to be used. Knowing your expenses with certainty you will be able to deduct more since you will have the necessary documents to justify the discounts, such as mileage for trips, use of cell phones, etc.

CONCLUSION

- Taxes are the way the State collects taxes and obtains most of the public income.

- We must bear in mind that taxes are divided into taxes, rates and special contributions.

- With taxes, the State is able to have sufficient resources to carry out actions such as infrastructure, administration or even the provision of services, among others.

- These taxes are paid by individuals, families or businesses to the State, and help meet the collective needs of the community, thus affecting the entire population in general.

- -In order to define what taxes are, it is necessary to understand that not all taxes are the same, since the amount to be paid in taxes varies depending on how much income they receive and how much property the people or companies that have to pay it have.

- Tax reductions are special measures applied by the States or the Congress of each nation with the objective of broadening the participation of citizens in contributing to the improvements and public expenditures of the nation.

- Reductions when you pay your income tax or ISR will benefit you as you plan in a timely and appropriate manner by keeping your receipts and statements up to date.

- Finally, a timely planning will optimize the distribution of your income thus allowing you to opt for the reduction of some of the payments to your taxes taking the appropriate provisions such as the use of spaces in the home.